Think Fast!!

A Beginner's Guide to Impromptu Speaking, Clear Thinking, and Concentration Skills

– **ARMANI**TALKS

CONTENTS

| Introduction

Why impromptu speak in the first place?
Isn't that the lazy person's skill?

As a matter of fact, no.
Impromptu speaking is a tool that will allow you to feel more confident in a variety of scenarios.

No one can truly think fast until there is some form of pressure. Anyone can think fast in the comfort of their home.

But a few people can think fast when their heart is beating fast, they aren't too sure if they will be able to pull the mission off, and they are terrified.

But they proceed forward anyways.

That's what the purpose of this book is about.

You will learn how to deal with pressure by willingly inviting in pressure.

One of the best ways to invite in pressure is by mastering impromptu speaking skills.

My name is Arman Chowdhury, the founder of ArmaniTalks.

ArmaniTalks is a media company that helps engineers and entrepreneurs improve their communication skills.

I relay my message through the vehicles of podcasting and YouTubing.

Want to know something?
The content in the ArmaniTalks YouTube channel and the ArmaniTalks Podcast are all impromptu talks. All I do is assign myself a topic, then I begin. No preparation ahead of time.

I've had someone ask me if I use a teleprompter. When I tell them there is no teleprompter, they look at me like I have 3 heads.

'Then how do you remember all that stuff?'

The question is not malicious.
It just shows that they believe talks need to be prepared beforehand. The concept of speaking off the cuff is something that does not exist for them.

For those who it does exist for, some view it as a lazy skillset.

I once had a Toastmaster buddy say:
'Yea, don't tell anyone you didn't prepare beforehand. It will be viewed in poor taste.'

I heard plenty of comments like this.
Then I wave off comments like this.

It's because impromptu speaking is a skill. A skill that can be learned, practiced, and mastered.

After recording over 400 YouTube videos, 400 podcasts, and having given 100s of Table Topics in Toastmasters, I have a few key principles that will spring you into action.

This book is pretty short.
I call it a micro book.
It has all the processes and frameworks to begin impromptu speaking.

This is a brand-new world to many. Once you step foot in this world, it becomes a **drug**.
Your mind has infinite potential. Now you will learn how to tame that infinite potential to create talks that will outlast you.
Let us begin.

– ARMANTALKS

Part 1:
| Definition

What is Impromptu Speaking?

> *Impromptu speaking is the art of creating talks without any preparation.*

When you look closely, you impromptu speak all the time!!

When you are talking to your best friend, are you planning what you are going to say?
'No.'
Then?
'I just say the first thing that comes to my mind.'

What if you are talking to your boss's, boss's, boss? Do you share the first thing that comes to your mind then?

'No!'

Why not?

'It's because that's my boss's, boss's, boss. If I say anything incorrect, then I may get fired!'

Therefore:

- At a relaxed state, we impromptu speak.
- At a tense state, we sound more rehearsed.

The goal of impromptu speaking is to do your best to relax. The better we relax, the better we create talks about what we already know.

No preparation needed.

Why Learn Impromptu Speaking?

You may be thinking:

'Why even learn this skillset? I have a lot on my plate already.'

Great question.
There are multiple uses for impromptu speaking. Here are a few…

| Reduced Speech Anxiety

One of the largest reasons for public speaking fear is because the speaker believes they are going to go on stage and forget what they practiced for.

They imagine themselves standing centerstage with the audience looking at them, disappointed.

Guess what?

If you are someone who knows impromptu speaking, then this fear is heavily reduced, or it doesn't exist at all.

There are a ton of impromptu speakers who are **happy** when they forget a point. This allows them to think on their feet and show others what they are made of.

Once you lose the fear of forgetting points, you'll see that a large amount of your speech anxiety melts away.

Now you can seamlessly:

- Deliver that best man speech.
- Deliver that presentation at work.
- And deliver what the hell you do for a living to your kid's classroom.

Reduced Social Anxiety

In 2007s, there was this famous show called the Pick-Up Artist. This was a show where Casanovas worked with a group of dorky men to teach them how to get better with women.

As the show progressed, there were a lot of tricks and lingo that were used.

One of the lingo's was:

- *Negging.*

You neg a woman by casually bringing up one of her flaws in a friendly way. The reason for this move is because it's a pattern interrupt that shows you aren't too needy.

Another lingo was:

- *Pickup line.*

This is a clever comment to break into the attractive woman's world.

Soon, multiple people began negging and doing pick-up lines.

In the initial stages, it was a refreshing way of doing things.
Later, it became stale and predictable.

These individuals eventually learned that rehearsing a conversation beforehand was **not** smart. That's because each interaction is different.

A large reason for social anxiety is from the fear that others will pull a fast one on us.

They will say something witty that has us stuttering.

This is another situation where impromptu speaking comes in clutch.

Knowing impromptu speaking is equivalent to becoming the guy who can fight. If you know how to fight, you don't go around fighting willy nilly. However, if you know how to fight, there is a level of calm that permeates your body language because you know you are **capable**.

Likewise, when knowing impromptu speaking, a part of you always feels **capable** of handling any social situation that is presented to you.

Reducing social anxiety in the process.

| Building Assets

I mentioned in the introduction that I have recorded 400+ YouTube videos and 400+ podcasts dealing with soft skills.

Want to know something?

Content is not subject to the laws of matter!
'English please...'
These content pieces will last **forever**.

These content pieces either promote other products of mine and/or give me money in the form of ad revenue.
'English please...'
The impromptu speaking skillset will build digital assets that pay me **forever.**

Others can do the same thing too. They can sharpen their impromptu speaking skillset to build their wealth overtime.

Ideas that lie in the mind, die in the mind.

So, share your ideas and watch your powers grow.

There are multiple ways to incorporate impromptu speaking into your life. You don't need to quit your job and become some comedian overnight.

Impromptu speaking allows for quick thinking, added rapport, and the ability to adjust on the fly.

Highly practical tools that can make anyone's life much better.

Part 2
Concentration

|Power of 1

With public speaking, one of the vital things to do is focus on 1 big idea.

The speaker thinks:

'Why would I focus on 1 idea? I can focus on 10. Don't believe me? Well, let me show you!!'

No one is saying that you can't do it. Instead, we are saying you shouldn't do it because you'll confuse the audience.

> ***In order to see the power of 1, you need to train the mind to think in themes.***

- *Dog.*
- *Cat.*
- *Mouse.*

These are 3 discrete words. If someone is focusing on the words, that means they will only see separateness.

But if I ask you:
What do all these 3 words have in common?
You'll be like:

- *Animal.*

Animal is the **theme** that unites these disparate words.

The reason being able to think in themes is important is because it allows the impromptu speaker to reverse engineer a talk into existence.

In a few of the future sections, I'm going to give you strategies to think in themes. But you can get a head start right now.

Are you into self-improvement?

You ever seen someone pick up random productive habits to only quit?

- They meditate.
- They go to the gym.
- They journal.

But they are just doing the acts. No theme behind those movements. No narrative.

Now imagine that the narrative was:
'I want to become the best version of myself and go on a competition with my prior day self for the rest of my life.'

Now there is a theme that brings those disparate acts to life!

In a conversation, when someone is telling you a story, just ask:
'What's the theme of what this person is trying to say?'
This will add much more clarity.

When watching a movie, aim to assess what the theme is:
'What is the gist that the filmmaker is try to transmit into me?'

Soon, when impromptu speaking, you will get a general theme and will have more than enough tools to begin.

Focus is the Natural State

We naturally are focus.
But overtime, we lost sight of that.

Imagine Billy has been wanting a new room for the longest time. Finally, he gets it.

In the beginning, he was taking so much care of his room.
It was spotless.

Later in the game, Billy began inviting his friends to chill in his room. They left wrappers, food, and other items on the floor.

The junk gradually added up. Billy lost focus of cleaning the room.

One day, Billy's mom comes and see's the room is a mess. It's so messy that she yells at him.

Having forgotten the initial state of the room, Billy tells his mom it was always dirty.

That's when his mom laughs and says: *'Shut up Billy and clean your room.'*

Our minds are like that too. We naturally are focus. Our mind is naturally clean. But overtime, it got dirty due to scrolling our phones without purpose, consuming junk in the media, and hanging out with negative people.

Impromptu speaking will allow you to clean your room.

I mean…. clean your mind.

From there, you will go back to the initial state of your mind being clear.

Congrats, clear thinking and concentration are in your future.

|Mind is a Muscle

As we progress in the book, I want you to think in terms of **increments**.

If you can't concentrate for more than 3 seconds, don't worry…

Start exactly where you are and gradually build up.

Neuroplasticity shows that the brain is constantly capable of wiring and firing new connections to reinvent itself.

You are not the same person now as you were 5 years ago.

We will start of light.
Focus on the foundations.
Then gradually pile brick by brick on top of that.

Part 3
| Challenges

Challenges to Expect

- When you don't expect something, you get rattled.
- When you expect something, you don't get rattled.

I'm going to give you some of the challenges from the beginning.

Impromptu speaking is going to feel very difficult.

At one point, you are thinking on hyperdrive trying to generate a talk. The next second, you find it difficult to breathe in a gentle pace as you are thinking and talking. While you are finding it difficult to think, talk, and breathe, there is soreness building from your neck, head, and arms.

What gives??
Why all the pain?

'I'm just speaking but it feels like I'm going to the gym!' you think.

This is what **all** impromptu speakers go through.
This is you retraining your body, mind, and breath towards 1 shared goal.

Right now, a person's body, mind, and breath are all over the place.

- Physically, they are present.
- Mentally, they are in la-la land.
- And their breath is choppy and far from smooth.

> **Impromptu speaking allows you to align all 3 variables towards a shared goal.**

This is you retraining the nervous system.
Very similar to driving.

Remember driving?
One second, you are trying to touch the steering wheel. The next moment, you have to toggle between the brake and the accelerator. The next moment, you have to look out for civilians.

So much!
No way can you balance all the variables.

But through practice, you reached a state of automatism.
'Automa-who??'
This is when you are capable of doing the task without any cognitive effort.
'Are you saying impromptu speaking will be like that?'

Yes. As long as you continue to make 1% progresses.

Which brings me to my next point…

1% Mindset = 1 Word Mindset

1 word recited to perfection is a lot in a creative field.

Rather than rushing through 50 sloppy words, get through 1 word to perfection.

Take it 1 word at a time if you feel that everything is feeling too difficult. This allows you to **ease** your way into learning this skillset.

The intent is to make incremental progress.

Sometimes, you'll be making progress in 2 things, but it feels like you are falling flat on 3 things.

All good.

Focus on the 2 things that you are doing well. That doesn't mean that you avoid understanding what you don't do well. Just focus on what you do well first, and this allows you to make more improvements over time.

Bottom line, since we are retraining ourselves on a being level, it becomes more important than ever to understand the power of 1% improvements.

In this field, no work goes to waste.

Give each word the respect that it deserves.

Part 4
Rule

#1 Rule of Impromptu Speaking

There's only 1 rule with impromptu speaking and 1 rule only:

- **DO NOT START OVER.**

Easier said than done, I get it.
However, this rule cannot be underestimated.
That's why it's the **only** rule!!

'What if I fumble, Armani? Should I start over then?'

No, do not start over.

There's something you should know….

The best ideas come from a state of unpredictability.

This is when you feel lost and have no clue how you are going to tie your present point to the theme of the talk. That's when your brain is firing and wiring new neural pathways that would have initially not been experienced!

Keep the talk going.
See where it takes you.

A lot of screenwriters operate like this. They LOVE it when they are lost. That's when they get to approach the story from a completely different angle. That's when they are connecting dots they initially didn't think of.

The one and only rule is to not start over.

Go through the fumbles.
When you fumble a word, your body will
feel a strong tension.
It's going to want to start over.
When you don't start over, that tension is
only going to get STRONGER AND
STRONGER.

Keep pushing.

Your body is making a note of the
uncomfortable feeling that you were feeling
for not starting over.

In the future, when you are about to fumble
again, there will be **micro** moves with your
lips and body language that prevents you
from making the same mistake.

What?

You thought your body wasn't noticing and adjusting?
You underestimate your nervous system.

Go through the discomfort.
The body will make notes.
It will adjust.

See where the talk takes you!!

Part 5
Strategies

Methods of Impromptu Speaking

In this section, you are going to learn a few frameworks of impromptu speaking.

Here's a suggestion:

- Pick **one** framework that resonates the most with you and go from good to great.

Avoid hopping around too much from framework to framework.

Overtime, once you feel like you have made significant progress in 1 path, then you can always expand to other paths.

The cool thing is when you are developing in 1 path, you will have the neural pathways of a budding impromptu speaker.
Which will allow you to pick up the other paths with ease.

Just be patient, my friend.
Hold onto one thing and make it strong.
Then add on.

|Basketball Method

Allow me to give you a few scenarios…

You are a basketball player.
You've been itching to play.

I give you a basketball and no hoop. How
will you feel?
'Eh, I won't feel too good.'
Why not?
'Because all I can do is dribble. I don't have
a hoop to shoot the ball through.'

Okay, let's flip this a little. Imagine if I give you the hoop and no ball, how would you feel?

'I'd feel worse. All I can do now is run and try to touch the hoop. Other than that, there's not much else to do.'

What if I give you a ball **and** a hoop, how you would you feel?

'I'd feel great! Now I can dribble and shoot.'

Impromptu speaking is the same way.

- Your words = You dribbling a ball.
- Your point is the hoop.

If you have words and no hoop, then you ramble.

If you have a hoop but no words, then you overthink.

But when you have a point **and** words?? Now you're unstoppable.

Rules for the Basketball Method:

1.   Pick the hoop.

That's the only rule. You generating the words is the impromptu speaking process.

- A general hoop leads to a long talk.
- A specific hoop leads to a short talk.

So, if you have the hoop of *'hippos,'* then this will be a long talk.
You can talk about hippos for a long time! If you had a seminar on hippos coming up, then you can use a general hoop.

But let's say you need a short talk to upload to your LinkedIn.
Then a specific hoop like:
'Explain why hippos are more dangerous than elephants.'
Will lead to a shorter talk because it is more hyper targeted.

You can get more targeted if need be.

'Explain why hippos are more dangerous than elephants and make the talk funny.'

Get creative.

|String and Pearls

- The string is the theme of the talk.
- The pearls are the main points of the talk.

<u>Rules for the String and Pearls Method:</u>

1. Create a string.

2. Think of a few pearls before or during the talk.

3. Begin.

Look at a pearl necklace.
Without the string, the pearls are all over the place.

Without the pearls, the string has no value.
But when you have the string and pearls, now you can create compelling jewelry.
Jewelry that's worth millions!!
Aka: your talk.

The best way to handle this framework is by being a big picture thinker. You don't want to be too detailed when using this framework. You can be more detailed once you begin the talk.

Let's say I give you an impromptu speech topic of:
'Explain a tough moment that you overcame.'
I provided the string for you.

Without much planning, what are some general pearls you can think of?

- Pearl 1: First car accident.
- Pearl 2: How I dealt with the car accident.

- Pearl 3: How I overcame the car accident.

These 3 pearls are not so detailed that you get lost in your head.

Get in the habit of thinking in strings and it will be easier to rest the pearls upon the string.

|Pink Fish Method

Imagine there is a crystal-clear lake that you can see through.
The lake is flowing in 1 direction.
Within this lake are a bunch of gray fish.
Boring....

But every now and then, there is a pink fish that swims by.
Your goal is to collect as many pink fishes as you can.

Sometimes, you will attempt to catch a pink fish, but you accidentally grab a gray fish instead.
Other times, you will catch the pink fish.

The **process** of getting your hand and reaching into the water is what builds the skillset.

The analogies are:

- The 1 direction of the lake is the theme of your talk.
- The gray fishes are the average thoughts floating in your mind.
- The pink fish is a thought that is fueled with emotion.
- The process of reaching in the water and grabbing the fish is like you reaching in your mind and capturing your ideas.

<u>Rules for the Pink Fish Method:</u>

1. Create a direction for your talk.

2. Allow your mind to generate thoughts.

> 3.   Capture only the thoughts that spark a physical sensation in the body.

When practicing this exercise, start off with topics that are **personal** to you.

The more personal it is to you, the more you will be able to spot the pink fish.

If you begin to speak about stop signs but stop signs don't have too much of a personal connection to you, then every thought will feel like a gray fish.

But let's say you didn't stop at a stop sign and got a ticket recently, now your narrative mind is engaged.
It's personal to you.

Without a theme for your talk, that's like a lake that has no direction. The fishes are going all over the place. It'll feel impossible to catch any of them.

So, create a theme for your talk that is personal to you.
Then catch as many pink fishes as you can!

|Machine Gun

You may have been reading these past few frameworks with a glazed look over your eyes.

You're the kind of person that doesn't like rules…*at all.*

If that's the case, then the machine gun method is for you.

Rules for the Machine Gun Method:

1.   Pick any topic and begin talking on it.

A lot of rappers do this. They begin with an idea and start freestyling. That's when they begin surprising themselves.

'Is this method efficient?'
It can be. But with this method, you are much more prone to rambling.

Therefore, self-awareness is key.

All ideas seem like a good idea when you have 0 idea of what to say.

At the beginning, there is a lot of disorder. But the more you practice, the disorder reduces and there is more order.

To practice, just pick a topic and begin to notice things on it.
As you notice things, you will notice possible conflicts.

Like a wallet.

- Who decided to call it a wallet?
- Who said it needed to be put in a pocket?

- Whose bright idea was it to create a pocket?

You started off in 1 lane of wallets, then found yourself in another lane of pockets.

See where the talk takes you.

Bottom line, you are speaking without preparation.
Therefore, machine gun off ideas and see which sticks.

Part 6
Practice

|How to Practice

It's one thing to be interested in impromptu speaking, it's another thing to bring the concepts to life through practice.

To practice, there are different methods. It can be formal or informal.

Formal is when you set aside time to practice. Informal is when you are going about your day and decide to pick up some impromptu speaking.

Let's start with formal.

|Formal Method

In this section, I will give you a few ideas to schedule time to practice impromptu speaking.

Private/Public YouTube Channel

A lot of people have no clue that making a private YouTube channel is a thing. I'm here to tell you it is a thing.

You just upload the video and don't make it public. You can always make it public later.

If you don't feel ready to have eyeballs watching you, keep it private and watch it yourself. The cool thing about the YouTube method is that you get to build a routine of recording and watching yourself back.

> **The ability to watch yourself back leads to stunning progress in the impromptu speaking journey.**

It's a cheatcode. Something that we will be discussing more in section 8.

Setting up a YouTube channel is pretty easy. Recording videos can be done on your phone. You can practice with the time limit that you see best fit.

I post 3 videos a week (Monday, Wednesday, and Friday). Talks hover around the 10-minute mark.

Podcast

A remix to the YouTube channel is a podcast. This is when you buy a USB mic and download Audacity (audio recording tool).

Find a few topics and articulate your ideas out loud. Practice doing the talks with any of the frameworks that you are the most comfortable with.

I post 3 podcasts a week (Tuesday, Thursday, and Saturday). Talks hover around the 6-minute mark.

Create a podcast where you soon become your number 1 fan.

Toastmaster Table Topics

Toastmasters is a public speaking club that helps all walks of life develop their communication skills.

One part of the club is the Table Topics portion. This is when the member is chosen by the Table Topics master and given a random topic. The member creates a 1-3 minute talk on the topic.

A lot of Toastmaster's clubs record these talks. If they don't record the talk, then you can just give someone your phone to record you.

The ability to speak when eyeballs are looking at you builds pressure like none other. Willingly inviting in pressure is a fantastic way to learn the skillset much quicker.

|Informal Method

The informal method can be done in a car ride or while having a conversation with someone.

You may be like:

- 'Hm... I talk in the car all the time without preparation.'

Or

- 'I talk to my friends all the time without planning what I'm going to say.'

You do!
Therefore, make yourself **aware**.

A big part of impromptu speaking is knowing that you already do it.

With your friend, I'm sure you are talking about a lot of topics that are pure impromptu. Make yourself **aware**, and see how your voice sounds, how relaxed you feel, and how present you are.

With the car rides…. here's the thing…
I call this baby impromptu speaking.

Normally in car rides, someone starts off in one topic and finds themselves in a brand-new topic.

This could be like the machine gun framework for impromptu speaking if there was some substance.

Do your best to stay on track.
If you want to switch points, then earn the transition!!

Don't just talk about:

- How sad you are.
- Then talk about the zoo out of nowhere.

Transition, my friend.

'You know, I've been feeling really sad recently. One thing that I used to do as a kid was go to the zoo with my dad when I was sad (transition). Guess I will go to the zoo.'

With a few timely transitions, you'll see you're closer to impromptu speaking than you initially thought.

Part 7
| Transformation

Monitoring Progress

Content is king.
I'm sure you have heard these 3 words
plenty of times. The reason why?
Because it's true.

You know that Tesla doesn't consider itself
a car company?
They consider themselves a data company.

When their cars are on the road driving
smoothly (or not so smoothly) the data is
being tracked and uploaded to shared servers
so future Tesla cars can have a smooth
driving experience.

Our version of data is content.

This is why you should be consuming your content back.
Whether it's the videos from your YouTube channel, listening to your podcasts, or seeing your Toastmasters Table Topics talks.

> ***What separates regular practice from deliberate practice is a feedback system.***

A feedback system allows you to objectify yourself.

One type of feedback system is a coach. Another type of feedback system is information technology.

In this book, our feedback system of choice is information technology (videos & podcasts).

Content is king.

We feed the content into our nervous
system.
Keep what worked.
Discard what doesn't.
Refine like none other.

How to Consume Content

Great sports players watch their film back. This is based on the psychoneuromuscular theory.

The definition of the theory on Google is:

> *The use of mental imagery of an activity can improve the motor performance of that activity. It states that, during the processing of imagery, the brain sends impulses to the muscles.*

Which means that watching your content back leads to significant changes in the mind and nervous system.

In order to watch film back, or listen to your audio back, there are a few things to look out for.

The first…

Gestalt Principle

Avoid getting too analytical.
Like:

- *'I should have used this word instead of that word.'*
- *'Why does my eyebrow look raised in this scene and not that scene?'*
- *'Why did I run out breath with this word?'*

Not saying that being detailed is bad. But for this field, generalities beat specificities. Just consume the content and go for the gestalt of things.

Gestalt is defined on Google as:
An organized whole that is perceived as more than the sum of its parts.

One way to do the gestalt principle properly is to listen to your body.

- When a word was said in a strange way, the body will alert you.
- When you loved the delivery of a certain point, the body will alert you.

Do You Like You?

Once you are done consuming the content, just ask:
'Do I like me?'

I'll be real.
When I first started consuming my content, I didn't really like me. I was doing my best

during the recording sessions. But during the watching sessions, I was like:
'Eh, I don't really like this dude.'

This is a completely normal problem to have.
Simply being a little aware leads to gargantuan changes in the long run.

Soon, you start to tell more jokes, smile more, and loosen up your face. You'll look forward to consuming your content back.

Versatility in Topics

Another thing you want to monitor over time is versatility of topics. Are you versatile or are you talking about the same thing most of the time?

In addition to versatility:

- How's the delivery?
- Is it logical?

- Are you a good storyteller?

Avoid being too analytical. Just look at the big picture and occasionally ask yourself these questions.

Watch Your Old Content Back

One great way to improve is to watch your **old** content. Like the first videos you ever recorded. This is why building a catalogue is so important, whether it's private or public.

You'll notice that when you see a transformation of:

- Where you were -> where you are now.

You feel more reinvigorated with the impromptu speaking process.

When I'm losing motivation, I look at my talks from April 2019 and I'm like:

'Whoa, I've come a long way!'

But I'm not always insulting my past self.
Sometimes, I'll notice my past self doing
something where I'm like:
*'Hey, how come you don't sneak in more
jokes to your talks like you used to?'*

Old content can help you see how much you
improved and see how much you can
incorporate past moves into the present.

Part 8
Bonus

|Additional Tactics

This section is completely optional.

> ***To speed up your impromptu speaking journey, having a simple reading and writing practice helps tremendously.***

Why?

It's because impromptu speaking is a game of catching ideas and expressing it in words.

When you read and write, this allow for you to think in words.

This makes it much easier to have a faster reaction rate when you are thinking of ways to express yourself.

Reading and writing doesn't have to be too advanced from the get-go. Remember…this book preaches the 1% improvement mindset.

When cultivating a practice, see if you can be consistent with it 50 years from now.

^This command automatically cuts through the fluff and allows you to build the right practice for the context of your life.

| A sample practice is:

- Get a Twitter and write 1-3 tweets a day.
- Read for 15 minutes a day.

You can even combine the 2.
Read the tweets you wrote.

Reading and writing will lead to improvement in impromptu speaking because you become a supreme linguist.

Conclusion

Before, I used to get angry when I just got done paying attention to someone and they wouldn't return the same courtesy.

Then I looked these people in the eyes. Their mind was so scattered that they were not capable of focusing even if they tried.

Nowadays, I don't hate on these people.
I empathize with them.

Concentration is more important than ever because it is scarcer than ever.

So much content is getting shorter and shorter.
Each content piece is vying for someone's attention.
Shredding their focus even more...

The thing with meditation is that some people just cannot be consistent with it. They know of the practical benefits but are like:

'I see what you're saying, but it's just not my thing bro.'

This is when impromptu speaking comes in clutch.
It's a form of meditation with your eyes open.

You get to:

- Know your thoughts.
- Collect your thoughts.
- Articulate your thoughts.

Thoughts are no longer something you identify with. Rather, thoughts become a tool that will allow you to build:

- Social connections.
- Digital assets.

- Compelling ideas that drive change.

It's just a game of adding the 1%'s up. Soon, you'll see the mind, body, and breath linking into 1.

> **You'll find your talks getting more nuanced, entertaining and effortless.**

Others ask you which teleprompter you are reading from. You smile and look back at them:
*'No teleprompter, my friend. I just learned the art of **thinking fast**.'*

If you enjoyed this book on impromptu speaking and want to know more about the ArmaniTalks brand, be sure to check out my website:

- www.armanitalks.com

In this website, you'll get a lot of my blogs, books, videos, and podcasts on topics ranging from public speaking, social skills, emotional intelligence and much more.

I also run a daily newsletter where I share short stories on how to be more articulate with words. Join the tribe for exclusive information here:

- www.armanitalks.com/newsletter

Good luck on sharpening this skillset.
The mind is a muscle.
Make it strong!

Get To The Point

A Beginner's Guide to Essay Writing, Critical Thinking Skills & Logical Reasoning

---

Get to the Point is a beginner's guide on how to write essays, use critical thinking, and break down complex topics with the use of logical analysis. Essays are a profound way to build your body of work and solidify your philosophy. Learn the art and science of essay writing in this book.

In Get to the Point, you will learn:

- How to create a compelling subject for your essays.
- The use of logic, words, and critical thinking to break down complex topics.
- Effective strategies to research your topic.
- A quick way to build a to build a rough draft.
- A simple framework for editing your essays to sound more conversational.
- The art of proofreading.
- How to overcome imposter syndrome and publish your work.
- Strategic ways to grow your digital empire with the use of essays.